MW01294598

Interpreting
Dr3AM5

Basic Dream Interpretation

D	R	E	A	M	S
R	E	S	P	E	U
E	V	S	P	S	B
A	E	E	L	S	L
M	A	N	I	A	I
S	L	T	C	G	M
		I	A	E	I
		A	B	S	N
		L	L		A
			E		L
					L
					Y

Kathy L. Campbell

ISBN: 1492865591
ISBN-13: 978-1492865599

DEDICATION

This book is dedicated to all those who believe God
still speaks in dreams and visions in the night!

TABLE OF CONTENTS

FORWARD

We in the Western world as a whole, have not given much credence or significance to dreams. The church in particular has pointed people away from there being any significance to our dreams. In some places if a person were to say to their spiritual leaders that God had spoken to them and given them direction through a dream, they would be dismissed as being flaky. But thanks be to God there is a fresh wind of God's Spirit blowing upon the Church and we are once again seeing that God does indeed speak to us through dreams and visions just as the Bible says will happen in the last days.

Acts 2:17-21
17'And it shall come to pass in the last days, says God, That I will pour out of My Spirit on all flesh; Your sons and your daughters shall prophesy, Your young men shall see visions, Your old men shall dream dreams. 18 And on My menservants and on My maidservants I will pour out My Spirit in those days; And they shall prophesy. 19 I will show wonders in heaven above And signs in the earth beneath: Blood and fire and vapor of smoke.
20 The sun shall be turned into darkness,
And the moon into blood, Before the coming of the great and awesome day of the LORD. 21 And it shall come to pass That whoever calls on the name of the LORD Shall be saved.' NKJV

Some would suggest that this is some new doctrine sweeping the church, but this has happened from the very beginning of the recording of Scripture. We see

Daniel as one who understood visions and dreams and interpreted them.

Dan 1:17-18
17 As for these four young men, God gave them knowledge and skill in all literature and wisdom; and Daniel had understanding in all visions and dreams. NKJV

God spoke to Joseph through dreams and he was promoted second to Pharaoh because of this ability. Not everyone was happy with Joseph's dreams however.

Gen 37:8-11
8 And his brothers said to him, "Shall you indeed reign over us? Or shall you indeed have dominion over us?" So they hated him even more for his dreams and for his words. 9 Then he dreamed still another dream and told it to his brothers, and said, "Look, I have dreamed another dream. And this time, the sun, the moon, and the eleven stars bowed down to me." 10 So he told it to his father and his brothers; and his father rebuked him and said to him, "What is this dream that you have dreamed? Shall your mother and I and your brothers indeed come to bow down to the earth before you?" 11 And his brothers envied him, but his father kept the matter in mind. NKJV

Though his family dismissed Joseph's dreams, there came a time when God would call upon the dreamer to interpret another's dream. The ability to discern what God was saying through dreams opened incredible doors for Joseph. Eventually this ability led to the fulfillment of the dream he had as a youth!

Gen 41:8
8 Now it came to pass in the morning that his spirit was troubled, and he sent and called for all the magicians of Egypt and all its wise men. And Pharaoh told them his dreams, but there was no one who could interpret them for Pharaoh. NKJV

Gen 41:12-13
12 Now there was a young Hebrew man with us there, a servant of the captain of the guard. And we told him, and he interpreted our dreams for us; to each man he interpreted according to his own dream. NKJV

God also spoke to king Saul through dreams and then stopped when Saul was in sin by not doing what God had instructed him to do.

1 Sam 28:6
6 And when Saul inquired of the LORD, the LORD did not answer him, either by dreams or by Urim or by the prophets. NKJV

1 Sam 28:15-16
15 Now Samuel said to Saul, "Why have you disturbed me by bringing me up?" And Saul answered, "I am deeply distressed; for the Philistines make war against me, and God has departed from me and does not answer me anymore, neither by prophets nor by dreams. Therefore I have called you, that you may reveal to me what I should do." NKJV

Solomon received the wisdom that made him famous through a dream.

1 Kings 3:5-15
5 At Gibeon the LORD appeared to Solomon in a dream by night; and God said, "Ask! What shall I give you?" 6 And Solomon said: "You have shown great mercy to Your servant David my father, because he walked before You in truth, in righteousness, and in uprightness of heart with You; You have continued this great kindness for him, and You have given him a son to sit on his throne, as it is this day. 7 Now, O LORD my God, You have made Your servant king instead of my father David, but I am a little child; I do not know how to go out or come in. 8 And Your servant is in the midst of Your people whom You have chosen, a great people, too numerous to be numbered or counted. 9 Therefore give to Your servant an understanding heart to judge Your people, that I may discern between good and evil. For who is able to judge this great people of Yours?" 10 The speech pleased the LORD, that Solomon had asked this thing. 11 Then God said to him: "Because you have asked this thing, and have not asked long life for yourself, nor have asked riches for yourself, nor have asked the life of your enemies, but have asked for yourself understanding to discern justice, 12 behold, I have done according to your words; see, I have given you a wise and understanding heart, so that there has not been anyone like you before you, nor shall any like you arise after you. 13 And I have also given you what you have not asked: both riches and honor, so that there shall not be anyone like you among the kings all your days. 14 So if you walk in My ways, to keep

My statutes and My commandments, as your father David walked, then I will lengthen your days." 15 Then Solomon awoke; and indeed it had been a dream. And he came to Jerusalem and stood before the ark of the covenant of the LORD, offered up burnt offerings, offered peace offerings, and made a feast for all his servants. NKJV

God appeared to the Joseph of the New Testament, and gave him instructions to take Mary as his wife. A dream also was given to Joseph to instruct him to flee into Egypt. Still another dream provided Joseph direction to him on when to return from Egypt.

Matthew 1:20
20 But while he thought about these things, behold, an angel of the Lord appeared to him in a dream, saying, "Joseph, son of David, do not be afraid to take to you Mary your wife, for that which is conceived in her is of the Holy Spirit. NKJV

Matthew 2:13
13 Now when they had departed, behold, an angel of the Lord appeared to Joseph in a dream, saying, "Arise, take the young Child and His mother, flee to Egypt, and stay there until I bring you word; for Herod will seek the young Child to destroy Him." NKJV

Matthew 2:19
19 But when Herod was dead, behold, an angel of the Lord appeared in a dream to Joseph in Egypt, NKJV

Matthew 2:22
22 But when he heard that Archelaus was reigning over Judea instead of his father Herod, he was afraid to go there. And being warned by God in a dream, he turned aside into the region of Galilee. NKJV

The Bible is clear that God speaks to us through dreams. The Scriptures also state that the interpretation belongs to God. We must be open to hear His voice in our dreams!

Genesis 40:8
8 And they said to him, "We each have had a dream, and there is no interpreter of it." And Joseph said to them, "Do not interpretations belong to God? Tell them to me, please." NKJV

John 10:27
27 My sheep hear My voice, and I know them, and they follow Me. NKJV

I want to include one last passage taken from Job in the Message Bible. It is a great key for the purpose of dreams.

Job 33:14-18
14 God always answers, one way or another,
even when people don't recognize his presence.
15 "In a dream, for instance, a vision at night,
when men and women are deep in sleep,
fast asleep in their beds — 16 God opens their ears
and impresses them with warnings 17 To turn them
back from something bad they're planning,

from some reckless choice, 18 And keep them from an early grave, from the river of no return.[1]

I pray this book written by my wife and daughter, will be a great help and encouragement to you as you ponder your dreams and begin to glean the nuggets that God is depositing into your life through your dreams. "He who has ears, let him hear!" May God Bless and guide you through your dreams!

Dr. Robert B. Campbell

---

[1] *(from THE MESSAGE: The Bible in Contemporary Language © 2002 by Eugene H. Peterson. All rights reserved.)*

INTRODUCTION

Proverbs 25:2
It is the glory of God to conceal a matter, but the
glory of kings is to search out a matter.

The Lord speaks much more than we may realize.
Dreams are one way The Lord will speak to us.

In the cool of the day, The Lord came to speak with
Adam and Eve. That was then the norm. Each day
God still desires to speak to men and women whom
He created in His own image.

Many times, we can be unaware of the Lord speaking
to us. God speaks in many different forms.

-the Bible
-prayer
-people
-creation
-sounds
-colors
-surroundings
-songs
-movies
-television
-newspaper
-internet
-sports
-activities
-objects
-visions
-dreams

Hopefully this book will help you gain knowledge and wisdom as you continue or begin to allow God to speak to you in your dreams.

CHAPTER I
DREAMERS IN SCRIPTURE

Proverbs 25:2
It is the glory of God to conceal a matter, but the glory of kings is to search out a matter.

My feeling is that the Lord loves to give us help and hints to cause our journey here on earth, to flow in the current of His love and in His Spirit. I believe that dreams are one way the glory of The Lord is concealed. He desires for us to seek Him and His will through dreams.

Dreamers in the Scriptures-

~Abimelech
Genesis 20:3-8
But God came to Abimelech <u>in a dream</u> by night, and said to him, " Indeed you are a dead man because of the woman whom you have taken, for she is a man's wife." But Abimelech had not come near her; and he said, " Lord, will You slay a righteous nation also? Did he not say to me, " She is my sister '? And she, even she herself said, 'He is my brother. ' In the integrity of my heart and innocence of my hands I have done this." And God said to him <u>in a dream</u>, " Yes, I know that you did this in the integrity of your heart. For I also withheld you from sinning against Me; therefore I did not let you touch her. Now therefore, restore the man's wife; for he is a prophet, and he will pray for you and you shall live. But if you do not restore her, know that you shall surely die, you and all who are yours." So Abimelech rose early in the morning, called all his servants, and told all

these things in their hearing; and the men were very much afraid.

PURPOSE OF THE DREAM- to protect Abimelech from an unintentional sin and its consequences.

~**Jacob**
Genesis 28:11-17
So he came to a certain place and stayed there all night, because the sun had set. And he took one of the stones of that place and put it at his head, and he lay down in that place to sleep. <u>Then he dreamed</u>, and behold, a ladder was set up on the earth, and its top reached to heaven; and there the angels of God were ascending and descending on it. And behold, the Lord stood above it and said:"I am the Lord God of Abraham your father and the God of Isaac; the land on which you lie I will give to you and your descendants. Also your descendants shall be as the dust of the earth; you shall spread abroad to the west and the east, to the north and the south; and in you and in your seed all the families of the earth shall be blessed. Behold, I am with you and will keep you wherever you go, and will bring you back to this land; for I will not leave you until I have done what I have spoken to you." Then Jacob awoke from his sleep and said, " Surely the Lord is in this place, and I did not know it." And he was afraid and said, "How awesome is this place! This is none other than the house of God, and this is the gate of heaven!"

PURPOSE OF THE DREAM- to bring Jacob into covenant relationship.

~Jacob

Genesis 31:10-13

"And it happened, at the time when the flocks conceived, that I lifted my eyes and saw <u>in a dream</u>, and behold, the rams which leaped upon the flocks were streaked, speckled, and gray- spotted. Then the Angel of God spoke to me <u>in a dream</u>, saying, 'Jacob.' And I said, 'Here I am.' And He said, 'Lift your eyes now and see, all the rams which leap on the flocks are streaked, speckled, and gray- spotted; for I have seen all that Laban is doing to you. I am the God of Bethel, where you anointed the pillar and where you made a vow to Me. Now arise, get out of this land, and return to the land of your family.'"

PURPOSE OF THE DREAM- to show Jacob how to prosper.

~Laban

Genesis 31:22-24

And Laban was told on the third day that Jacob had fled. Then he took his brethren with him and pursued him for seven days' journey, and he overtook him in the mountains of Gilead. But God had come to Laban the Syrian <u>in a dream</u> by night, and said to him, "Be careful that you speak to Jacob neither good nor bad."

PURPOSE OF THE DREAM- to warn Laban not to cross a line with God.

~Joseph

Genesis 37:5-7

Now Joseph <u>had a dream</u>, and he told it to his brothers; and they hated him even more. So he said to them, *"Please hear this dream which I have dreamed: There we were, binding sheaves in the field. Then behold, my sheaf arose and also stood upright; and indeed your sheaves stood all around and bowed down to my sheaf."*

PURPOSE OF THE DREAM- to give Joseph a future.

~Joseph
Genesis 37:9-11
Then <u>he dreamed</u> still another dream and told it to his brothers, and said, "Look, I have dreamed another dream. And this time, the sun, the moon, and the eleven stars bowed down to me." So he told it to his father and his brothers; and his father rebuked him and said to him, "What is this dream that you have dreamed? Shall your mother and I and your brothers indeed come to bow down to the earth before you?" And his brothers envied him, but his father kept the matter in mind.

PURPOSE OF THE DREAM- to confirm Joseph's calling and future.

~The Baker and The Butler
Genesis 40:5-19
Then the butler and the baker of the king of Egypt, who were confined in the prison, <u>had a dream</u>, both of them, each man's dream in one night and each man's dream with its own interpretation. And Joseph came in to them in the morning and looked at them, and saw that they were sad. So he asked Pharaoh's officers who were with him in the custody of his lord's house, saying, "Why do you look so sad today?"

And they said to him, "We each have had a dream, and there is no interpreter of it." So Joseph said to them, "Do not interpretations belong to God? Tell them to me, please." Then the chief butler told his dream to Joseph, and said to him, " Behold, in my dream a vine was before me, and in the vine were three branches; it was as though it budded, its blossoms shot forth, and its clusters brought forth ripe grapes. Then Pharaoh's cup was in my hand; and I took the grapes and pressed them into Pharaoh's cup, and placed the cup in Pharaoh's hand." And Joseph said to him, "This is the interpretation of it:The three branches are three days. Now within three days Pharaoh will lift up your head and restore you to your place, and you will put Pharaoh's cup in his hand according to the former manner, when you were his butler. But remember me when it is well with you, and please show kindness to me; make mention of me to Pharaoh, and get me out of this house. For indeed I was stolen away from the land of the Hebrews; and also I have done nothing here that they should put me into the dungeon." When the chief baker saw that the interpretation was good, he said to Joseph, "I also was in my dream, and there were three white baskets on my head. In the uppermost basket were all kinds of baked goods for Pharaoh, and the birds ate them out of the basket on my head." So Joseph answered and said, "This is the interpretation of it:The three baskets are three days. Within three days Pharaoh will lift off your head from you and hang you on a tree; and the birds will eat your flesh from you."

PURPOSE OF THE DREAM- to make a Divine connection for Joseph.

~Pharaoh
Genesis 41:1-4
Then it came to pass, at the end of two full years, that Pharaoh <u>had a dream</u>; and behold, he stood by the river. Suddenly there came up out of the river seven cows, fine looking and fat; and they fed in the meadow. Then behold, seven other cows came up after them out of the river, ugly and gaunt, and stood by the other cows on the bank of the river. And the ugly and gaunt cows ate up the seven fine looking and fat cows. So Pharaoh awoke.

PURPOSE OF THE DREAM- to give Pharaoh a sign of what was to come.

~Pharaoh
Genesis 41:5-8
He slept <u>and dreamed</u> a second time; and suddenly seven heads of grain came up on one stalk, plump and good. Then behold, seven thin heads, blighted by the east wind, sprang up after them. And the seven thin heads devoured the seven plump and full heads. So Pharaoh awoke, and indeed, it was a dream. Now it came to pass in the morning that his spirit was troubled, and he sent and called for all the magicians of Egypt and all its wise men. And Pharaoh told them his dreams, but there was no one who could interpret them for Pharaoh.

PURPOSE OF THE DREAM- the plight of Egypt was sealed.

~A Midianite
Judges 7:12-15
Now the Midianites and Amalekites, all the people of the East, were lying in the valley as numerous as locusts; and their camels were without number, as the sand by the seashore in multitude. And when Gideon had come, there was a man telling <u>a dream</u> to his companion. He said, "I have had a dream: To my surprise, a loaf of barley bread tumbled into the camp of Midian; it came to a tent and struck it so that it fell and overturned, and the tent collapsed." Then his companion answered and said, " This is nothing else but the sword of Gideon the son of Joash, a man of Israel! Into his hand God has delivered Midian and the whole camp." And so it was, when Gideon heard the telling of the dream and its interpretation, that he worshiped. He returned to the camp of Israel, and said, " Arise, for the Lord has delivered the camp of Midian into your hand."

PURPOSE OF THE DREAM- to put the fear of God into the Midianites and to prove to Gideon that God was with him and would give him victory.

~Solomon
1 Kings 3:4-15
Now the king went to Gibeon to sacrifice there, for that was the great high place:Solomon offered a thousand burnt offerings on that altar. At Gibeon the Lord appeared to Solomon <u>in a dream</u> by night; and God said, " Ask! What shall I give you?" And Solomon said:"You have shown great mercy to Your servant David my father, because he walked before You in truth, in righteousness, and in uprightness of heart with You; You have continued this great kindness for

him, and You have given him a son to sit on his throne, as it is this day. Now, O Lord my God, You have made Your servant king instead of my father David, but I am a little child; I do not know how to go out or come in. And Your servant is in the midst of Your people whom You have chosen, a great people, too numerous to be numbered or counted. Therefore give to Your servant an understanding heart to judge Your people, that I may discern between good and evil. For who is able to judge this great people of Yours?" The speech pleased the Lord, that Solomon had asked this thing. Then God said to him:"Because you have asked this thing, and have not asked long life for yourself, nor have asked riches for yourself, nor have asked the life of your enemies, but have asked for yourself understanding to discern justice, behold, I have done according to your words; see, I have given you a wise and understanding heart, so that there has not been anyone like you before you, nor shall any like you arise after you. And I have also given you what you have not asked:both riches and honor, so that there shall not be anyone like you among the kings all your days. So if you walk in My ways, to keep My statutes and My commandments, as your father David walked, then I will lengthen your days." Then Solomon awoke; and indeed it had been a dream. And he came to Jerusalem and stood before the ark of the covenant of the Lord, offered up burnt offerings, offered peace offerings, and made a feast for all his servants.

PURPOSE OF THE DREAM- to give a gift of wisdom.

~Solomon

1 Kings 9:1-9

And it came to pass, when Solomon had finished building the house of the Lord and the king's house, and all Solomon's desire which he wanted to do, that <u>the Lord appeared to Solomon the second time, as He had appeared to him at Gibeon</u>. And the Lord said to him:"I have heard your prayer and your supplication that you have made before Me; I have consecrated this house which you have built to put My name there forever, and My eyes and My heart will be there perpetually. Now if you walk before Me as your father David walked, in integrity of heart and in uprightness, to do according to all that I have commanded you, and if you keep My statutes and My judgments, then I will establish the throne of your kingdom over Israel forever, as I promised David your father, saying, 'You shall not fail to have a man on the throne of Israel.' But if you or your sons at all turn from following Me, and do not keep My commandments and My statutes which I have set before you, but go and serve other gods and worship them, then I will cut off Israel from the land which I have given them; and this house which I have consecrated for My name I will cast out of My sight. Israel will be a proverb and a byword among all peoples. And as for this house, which is exalted, everyone who passes by it will be astonished and will hiss, and say, 'Why has the Lord done thus to this land and to this house?' Then they will answer, 'Because they forsook the Lord their God, who brought their fathers out of the land of Egypt, and have embraced other gods, and worshiped them and served them; therefore the Lord has brought all this calamity on them. '"

PURPOSE OF THE DREAM- to serve as a reminder to faithfully follow The Lord.

~Job
Job 7:14
Then You scare me <u>with dreams</u> and terrify me <u>with</u>
<u>visions,</u>

~Nebuchadnezzar
Daniel 7:1
In the first year of Belshazzar king of Babylon,
Daniel <u>had a dream</u> and visions of his head while on
his bed. Then he wrote down the dream, telling the
main facts.

PURPOSE OF THE DREAM- to reveal what was to come.

~Joseph
Matthew 1:20-25
But while he thought about these things, behold, an
angel of the Lord appeared to him <u>in a dream</u>,
saying, " Joseph, son of David, do not be afraid to
take to you Mary your wife, for that which is
conceived in her is of the Holy Spirit. And she will
bring forth a Son, and you shall call His name Jesus,
for He will save His people from their sins."
So all this was done that it might be fulfilled which
was spoken by the Lord through the prophet, saying:
" Behold, the virgin shall be with child, and bear a
Son, and they shall call His name Immanuel," which
is translated, " God with us." Then Joseph, being
aroused from sleep, did as the angel of the Lord
commanded him and took to him his wife, and did

*not know her till she had brought forth her firstborn
Son. And he called His name Jesus.*

PURPOSE OF THE DREAM- to give Joseph
instruction, peace, and confirming Mary's story.

~**Joseph**
Matthew 2:13
*Now when they had departed, behold, an angel of the
Lord appeared to Joseph <u>in a dream</u>, saying, "Arise,
take the young Child and His mother, flee to Egypt,
and stay there until I bring you word; for Herod will
seek the young Child to destroy Him."*

PURPOSE OF THE DREAM- to save their lives.

~**Joseph**
Matthew 2:19-20
*Now when Herod was dead, behold, an angel of the
Lord appeared <u>in a dream</u> to Joseph in Egypt,
saying, "Arise, take the young Child and His mother,
and go to the land of Israel, for those who sought the
young Child's life are dead."*

PURPOSE OF THE DREAM- for direction.

~**Joseph**
Matthew 2:22
*But when he heard that Archelaus was reigning over
Judea instead of his father Herod, he was afraid to
go there. And being warned by God <u>in a dream</u>, he
turned aside into the region of Galilee.*

PURPOSE OF THE DREAM- to save their lives.

~The Wise Men
Matthew 2:7-12
Then Herod, when he had secretly called the wise men, determined from them what time the star appeared. And he sent them to Bethlehem and said, " Go and search carefully for the young Child, and when you have found Him, bring back word to me, that I may come and worship Him also."
When they heard the king, they departed; and behold, the star which they had seen in the East went before them, till it came and stood over where the young Child was. When they saw the star, they rejoiced with exceedingly great joy. And when they had come into the house, they saw the young Child with Mary His mother, and fell down and worshiped Him. And when they had opened their treasures, they presented gifts to Him: gold, frankincense, and myrrh. Then, being divinely warned <u>in a dream</u> that they should not return to Herod, they departed for their own country another way.

PURPOSE OF THE DREAM- to protect Jesus.

~Pilate's Wife
Matthew 27:15-19
Now at the feast the governor was accustomed to releasing to the multitude one prisoner whom they wished. And at that time they had a notorious prisoner called Barabbas. Therefore, when they had gathered together, Pilate said to them, " Whom do you want me to release to you? Barabbas, or Jesus who is called Christ?" For he knew that they had handed Him over because of envy. While he was sitting on the judgment seat, his wife sent to him, saying, "Have nothing to do with that just Man, for I

have suffered many things today in a dream because of Him."

PURPOSE OF THE DREAM- revelation of who Jesus is to Pilate's wife.

In the passage below, God has marked His prophets by the evidence of seeing visions, experiencing dreams and hearing from God in puzzles and riddles-

Numbers 12:6-8
Then He said, "Hear now My words: If there is a prophet among you, I, the Lord, make Myself known to him in a vision; I speak to him in a dream.
Not so with My servant Moses; He is faithful in all My house. I speak with him face to face, even plainly, and not in dark sayings; and he sees the form of the Lord. Why then were you not afraid to speak against My servant Moses?"

God speaks to us in dreams as stated in the below passage-

Job 33:14-16
For God may speak in one way, or in another, yet man does not perceive it. In a dream, in a vision of the night, when deep sleep falls upon men, while slumbering on their beds, then He opens the ears of men, and seals their instruction.

There will be an ever greater increase of revelation coming to us through our dreams in the last days.

Acts 2:17-21
'And it shall come to pass in the last days, says God,
that I will pour out of My Spirit on all flesh; Your
sons and your daughters shall prophesy, your young
men shall see visions, your old men **shall dream**
dreams. *And on My menservants and on My*
maidservants I will pour out My Spirit in those days;
and they shall prophesy. I will show wonders in
heaven above and signs in the earth beneath: Blood
and fire and vapor of smoke. The sun shall be turned
into darkness, and the moon into blood, before the
coming of the great and awesome day of the Lord.
And it shall come to pass that whoever calls on the
name of the Lord shall be saved.'

As stated above in the book of Acts, in the last days
there will be an increase of revelation. If the New
Covenant is greater than the Old Covenant, imagine
what the church will look like as the Holy Spirit is
poured out as is prophesied here.

Genesis is a foundational book that lays out so much
by way of principle and practice. There is at least fifty
times alone where dreams and visions are mentioned
in the book of Genesis. This is more than is mentioned
in the New Testament. If dreams and visions are
mentioned this much in the beginning of time, what
will it be like in the last days? In the last days...there is
increase.

CHAPTER II
MY PERSONAL THOUGHTS REGARDING DREAMS

Dreams are a very real means of communication from God to us and offer wisdom and guidance to the dreamer.

Why does God give dreams?
Simply because the Lord wants to.

Dreams occur when we are vulnerable and lack conscious control over our thoughts while we sleep. Dreams are a way for The Lord to bypass any resistance in us from receiving significant and important information. When we are awake, there is abundant activity and noise. Activities and busyness of the day can actually distract us from dwelling on a thought that The Lord might be emphasizing in order to bring us wisdom. We easily find ourselves moving throughout the day with little time to meditate on what God may have to say on any given subject. We may even feel confident that we know what God might say or feel about a situation or circumstance, etc. and then He brings a dream and really opens our understanding. Of course, many discount dreams as a means of hearing from God. Some despise and belittle dreams as a valid source of communication from The Lord and may even describe all or most dreams as coming from our own soul.

Does The Lord really give dreams as a means of communicating with us?

The Lord takes pleasure in having us search out the understanding whether on Scripture itself or even through a dream. He likes that we put our thoughts and attention on Him and what He is communicating.

The Lord delights when we dig into a dream and discover hidden treasures of wisdom and help from Him. It is similar to when I see my grandbabies squeal with joy when they open a gift from me. I love to watch their faces when they see what is inside the bag or gift. The Lord wants us to unwrap our dreams to learn and enjoy from them as well.

Can you imagine if Joseph in the New Testament had disregarded the four dreams mentioned in the Scriptures? Or what if the Wise Men had ignored the dream of warning? Or even Abimelech? Or Laban? Or what if Solomon did not recognize the gift given to him in a dream? We can have gifts wrapped in beautiful paper all around us but until we open those gifts they will serve us no purpose. Dreams are like extra special gifts from The Lord. If one of my grand babies were to never open their gifts from me, eventually, I would stop bringing them gifts. Because they get so excited each time I give them a gift and cannot wait to see what the surprise holds, I am compelled to bring more gifts.

One way to approach dreams is to look for the wisdom being offered in the dream. He gives wisdom liberally to those who ask and one way God can give us wisdom is through our dreams. Let's not disregard or ignore our dreams, or even blame spicy pizza as a cause to dream. Instead, let's take note of our dreams and dig for the nuggets of wisdom God may be giving us.

Are all dreams from The Lord?

Are all dreams from God is a question asked many times over. The answer to this seems to be the excuse to not give heed to dreams. Once we determine that not all dreams are from God we find it easier to place a label over all or most dreams as being from our own soul. We must be careful that we are not giving ourselves more credit than we ought. The fact is God does give dreams. The fact is God gives wisdom to us in dreams. The fact is there will be an increase of dreams in the last days. Here is what I love about interpreting dreams. It causes me to look at Scriptures and pray. And I have found that as I draw near to God for an answer, He draws near to me. Amazing how the Scriptures work.

How about soul dreams?

Ecclesiastes 5:3
3 As a dream comes when there are many cares,
so the speech of a fool when there are many words.
NIV

Ecclesiastes 5:3
2 For nightmares come from worrying too much;
and a fool, when he speaks, chatters too much. CJB

We can see from the passages above that our thoughts, emotions, worries and concerns can have impact on our dreams. Our soul is our mind, will and emotions or our personality expressed. It is what we think, what we feel, who we are. Our dreams can be an expression of the soul when we are burdened down with the cares of life. These are not dreams from the enemy or even Godly dreams, but are dreams that show us where we are at in our journey towards becoming like Christ. The soul dream can represent the battle going on within us between the Holy Spirit and our flesh or carnal man. Once this type of dream is recognized, we need to respond in the appropriate way. We need to judge ourselves and allow God to chasten us as we get back on track with His will and way in our life.

1 Corinthians 11:31-32
31 For if we would judge ourselves , we would not be judged. 32 But when we are judged, we are chastened by the Lord, that we may not be condemned with the world. NKJV

Most of the time in going through a difficult situation it will cause me to draw closer to The Lord. Often during a worship service I draw near to The Lord. I have learned that whatever state that I am in, I have opportunity to draw near to God. So I intentionally look for The Lord all throughout the day and that includes meditating on my dreams. Without faith it is impossible to please The Lord. Faith is the substance of things hoped for and the evidence of things not seen. If I do not have hope that God will speak to me (including dreams) then I have no faith in the dreams.

My concern is not if God speaks through dreams but whether I want to know what is He speaking through dreams. Looking for ways The Lord speaks to us is one of the great joys as a believer.

What is the main or basic key to interpreting dreams?

The key to interpreting dreams is found in The Lord Himself and in His
Word. The Word is living and powerful. The key to every interpretation will be found either in His Word, in His Presence or having the Holy Spirit speak to you. This in and of itself is a lot of dwelling on The Lord and His Word.

Are dreams intrinsic or extrinsic?

It is very important that we understand that most dreams are about us. I believe that a vast majority of our dreams are intrinsic and deal with what is going on with you, changes in your life, relationships, God, the thoughts of your own heart, etc. Very few of our dreams are extrinsic, dealing with someone or someplace other than you.

Another key to interpreting dreams is to remember that The Lord is speaking to the dreamer and much of the symbolism will be related to the dreamer. I have interpreted dreams for about 20 years and found that I can give thoughts on what I perceive The Lord to be speaking but ultimately it has to resonate with the dreamer. For instance, in my dreams, dogs symbolize loyalty and friendship for me most of the time. But sometimes, I have had a dream of barking dogs which then symbolizes accusation. For someone else dreaming of dogs, it may symbolize fear or caution.

Remember, The Lord is speaking to the dreamer in a language they understand.

The method I use in interpreting dreams is to first pray and ask The Lord to reveal His wisdom from the dream. There are two main points I have gleaned through the years of interpreting dreams. First, there is always wisdom given in a dream. Secondly, The Lord often gives **warning, direction and correction** in dreams. If we dream of a grumpy old person it is probably revealing our own old grumpiness that The Lord wants to adjust in us. We might want to point a finger at the grumpy old person in church as though we are proving they have a bad attitude when in truth The Lord is wanting to help us out of our own bad attitude. The Lord uses people as symbolism many times. It is not so much about the person you dreamed about as much as it is about you.

Sometimes we get stuck on an individual in our dream and feel strongly that the dream is for them. I have learned to first apply the dream to myself and glean wisdom. A good rule of thumb is that if the dream is exposing sin in someone's life, first search your own heart to see if there be any sin in you. Sometimes we are blind to our own faults or sin. The principle is to first remove the log in our own eye. The Lord is so incredibly gracious and longing to help us draw closer to Him. Sin separates us from The Lord. It is a wonderful expression of the Father's love to give us a dream that reveals areas in our life where we fall short so that we can make the adjustment and draw closer to The Lord.

We can even have dreams about the church. Remember, that the church is called the bride of Christ. We are the bride of Christ. So, if we dream about the church having a lack of prayer or zeal for instance, it may be a revelation about you and your own personal life. Again, it is the love and mercy of God to show us how to draw closer to Him. I find that the Lord is always after my heart and the motives of my heart.

Most dreams are symbolic although there will be literal dreams as well. You might have a dream of walking to your car and seeing money from your wallet on the ground. You could interpret this as that you will recover anything of value that was lost or missing. The wisdom is to be alert and observant as The Lord is about to show you what you have been missing. However, this could also be a literal dream. Later on you will see "Charity's Corner" and read about a literal dream she once had.

In my observation, literal dreams are not typically dreams that reveal sin in someone else as much as they come to help someone discover a hidden secret or to reveal the love of The Lord for them or something of encouragement. In nearly every case where I have had literal dreams it has been a "life saving" type dream or one that lends wisdom from The Lord. In other words, I do not believe it to be the norm that The Lord will tell you a sin in someone else's life or to reveal a weakness. It appears that dreams meant for other people tend to be encouraging or exhorting or comforting.

How do we know if a dream is from The Lord for someone else?

One in a position of over sight or authority may have The Lord speak to them in a dream about someone within their own care who needs attention. This is so wonderful of The Lord to do for us.

If the dream changes the way we view someone or how we treat them then we need to evaluate our own heart and the motive of our own heart. Dreams from God are not meant to pit us against one another or against the church itself. Dreams from God are not meant to cause us to become suspicious of one another. Dreams from God are not meant to divide or separate.

In my prophetic training class, as well as my dream class, I instruct ones to speak well of others and encourage others in their walk with The Lord. Prophecy is for the edification, the exhortation, and the comfort of the church. I further instruct that if what you have to say to someone is not edifying then buy a roll of duct tape and tape your mouth closed. The Bible says to pursue love. Jesus laid out the first and greatest commandment and then told us the second is like unto it. Love is powerful. Love is believing the best in another person. Love is preferring the other person. Love is not selfish. So if we find ourselves dreaming of ways to "fix" other people, our own heart has deceived us.

Can anyone interpret dreams?

Anyone can cook but not all cook well. Anyone can interpret dreams but not all excel in interpreting dreams. If you use a "list of symbols" or a "manual" to interpret every dream you will become like canned food. There is good substance in canned food but no comparison to freshly made food. Allow The Lord to build your own understanding of your dreams.

Dream Interpretation is a skill to be learned. The more we practice the more God perfects us. If we are too occupied to spend time with God then we will not develop the gift of God within. I liken it to tuning in to a radio station. Until you find the right frequency there will be static and it will not be clear. The way to find the right frequency is by reason of use. All other stations must be tuned out to catch clearly what is said on that one station. This all takes time.

Does every person dream?

Yes, every person does dream. Memory is not the issue. All dream. At least that is what most of the research says. Here is a quote from Psychology Today.

> *"To really be sure that an individual does not dream we would have to follow him for years and perform awakenings from REM sleep to see if he dreamed. If the individual never reported a dream after years of awakenings from REM sleep then we could reasonably conclude that either the person does not dream or that he lacks the ability to recall dreams or that he is a liar (for some*

reason he wants to conceal the fact that he does in fact dream)."[2]

And this from Web MD

During sleep, the body cycles between non-REM and REM sleep. Typically, people begin the sleep cycle with a period of non-REM sleep followed by a very short period of REM sleep. Dreams generally occur in the REM stage of sleep.[3]

Why do we not remember our dreams?

There can be a few reasons we don't remember our dreams.

1- We have been taught that dreams are irrelevant or unimportant and therefore, we really have trained our minds not to remember them. This is easy to correct. Repent of an indifferent attitude towards dreams.

2- We may not want to hear from God and therefore, do not remember our dreams.

3- The alarm going off in the morning causes us to jump start our day. You might try waking up quietly before the alarm and ask The Lord if He spoke to you during the night.

We must first give value to our dreams and in so doing will begin to recall our dreams.

---

[2] http://www.psychologytoday.com/blog/dream-catcher/201204/people-who-do-not-dream

[3] http://www.webmd.com/sleep-disorders/excessive-sleepiness-10/sleep-101

Years ago, my son Josiah, said that it is really easy to dream. He went on to say that all you have to do is relax and invite the peace of God in before going to sleep. I have thought of this many times and realize that within this statement is first, the acknowledgement that God speaks through dreams and secondly, peace is a form of trust. When we walk in peace it is because we trust The Lord. I desire all that The Lord has for me and I desire for Him to speak to me even if it is within a dream. I trust The Lord to not give me a stone if I ask Him for a piece of bread. Walking in peace is key.

Should I write my dreams down?

Another key to recalling our dreams is in taking the responsibility for them. Writing the dream down and meditating on the Lord is being responsible for the information given through the dream. You will find that you begin to recall more of your dreams when you take responsibility for them. You may want to have a journal or notebook by the bedside for recording your dreams. Many times we awake from a dream and we are convinced we will not forget it by morning. Unfortunately, many of these dreams are lost. The best practice is to record it immediately.

Is it important how many dreams I have?

The amount of dreams we have is not what is important. Occasionally I will go for a long length of time where I do not recall my dreams when in fact I know I did dream. It is crucial to acknowledge that God will speak to us in dreams and not look down on dreams. Both Daniel and Ezekiel had understanding of metaphors and that God does speak to us in dreams and visions. It is important to note that God does speak through dreams, regardless of whether we have previously acknowledge that or not.

What types or kinds of dreams are there?

There are many different kinds of dreams. One kind is a dream of healing. I will give you an example. One night I went to bed sick to my stomach. After going to sleep I had a dream in which an angel from The Lord came and laid hands on my stomach for healing. When I awakened, my stomach still hurt until I thanked The Lord for sending the angel to release healing. At that moment I was totally pain free and healed. Faith is required to believe God speaks to us in dreams, and faith is required to activate healing when that is the message in the dream. This is so important to understand. Obviously, if you do not believe that God will speak through a dream, then you can miss an opportunity for healing.

Here are a few types of dreams you might have- healing, warning, correction, intercession, direction, body (through being pregnant or physical illness), calling dreams, invention type dreams, spiritual warfare, revelation, fear, chemical (occur through the taking of drugs whether over the counter, prescription or illegal), and others.

I will give an example of a chemical dream. We were called to the hospital by a friend who suffered from an asthma attack. When we got to the room of this friend, they had just awakened from a dream of spiders covering their entire body. This individual was concerned and fearful that there may be an assignment of witchcraft against them. We pointed out that the taking of any drug can induce fear type of dreams. Once we prayed and commanded all fear to leave, the individual was able to rest in peace and gained new understanding of the activity of drugs in the body and what they can create.

Treasure your dreams.

I absolutely love when the Lord speaks to me through a dream. One night I had a dream where The Lord asked me what I wanted Him to do for me. In the dream I knew this was a similar dream to the one Solomon had (*1 Kings 3:5-15*). Without thinking, I answered with wanting my children to radically love and serve the Lord. Then I awakened and felt so disappointed in myself for not asking for wisdom until I realized that the Lord filled my mouth with the correct answer as he did with Solomon. I now treasure this experience.

My desire is that this book helps you in gaining greater appreciation and understanding of your dreams. I have added a section on symbols to help bring some understanding to your dreams. You can add your own to the symbols I have offered. Be careful and intentional to build your own vocabulary and understanding for yourself. God is speaking to you in your symbolic language. The Think Tank at the back of the book will help to expand your understanding. Just start by getting the thinking cap on and listening for the Lord.

CHAPTER III
INTERPRETING DREAMS

The most basic way to interpret dreams is to ask the Holy Spirit to teach you, as interpretation is a byproduct of a relationship with The Lord.

The interpretation of dreams can come in one of these five ways-
    1- The interpretation comes while you dream
    2- The interpretation comes as you write the dream down
    3- The interpretation comes as you "go your way"- ponder on it
    4- The interpretation comes through mature or seasoned dream interpreters
    5- The Lord sends an angel to reveal the interpretation

Example-
I dream that it is raining outside- a very heavy rain.

First, ask the Holy Spirit to help you understand what the dream means.

Secondly, glean from the feelings you experienced in the dream. If you were fearful in the dream and recalled a flood from past years, it may be an indication of you facing a fear in your life at the present, or it could be a warning of difficult times ahead.

Thirdly, pick up a concordance and search for the word, rain. In this verse, rain can speak of teaching.

Deuteronomy 32:2
Let my teaching drop as the rain, My speech
distill as the dew, As raindrops on the tender herb,
and as showers on the grass.

In these two verses, rain speaks of the Presence of The
Lord.

Psalms 72:6
He shall come down like rain upon the grass
before mowing, like showers that water the earth.

Hosea 6:3
   Let us know, let us pursue the knowledge of the
   Lord. His going forth is established as the
   morning; He will come to us like the rain, like
   the latter and former rain to the earth.

When seeking the understanding of dreams we need
to consider these aspects:
   1- The "setting" of the dream
Where does the dream take place?
   2- The "characters" in the dream
Who is in your dream and what do these characters
mean to you?
   3- The "plot" or the "bottom line" activity of the
dream
What is the activity in the dream?
   4- The "feelings or emotions of the dreamer" in the
dream
How did you feel in the dream? How did you feel
when you woke up?

What can help to find the meaning of your dreams is to build or create a dream journal where you write your dream down and then, just like in English class, we break the "story" down to discover the meaning. It might look something like this:

Dream-
A very large group of people were standing around a large in ground pool. The water was green and murky. You could not see to the bottom of the pool. A young girl of eight years, Zoe, jumped into the pool. I screamed, NO, because we could not see her to find her. Zoe came up out of the water with her head lifted up, hands at her side, and a clear coating on her. She looked beautiful and very mystical. I looked down and the water was clear as crystal.

In the dream I woke up (though I was still dreaming) and saw William Seymour walking to a church where he would be speaking. As he got to the church the door was padlocked. He was literally locked out of the church. He turned around to leave and I felt the deep disappointment and sadness of what had just happened. Then I began to recount the miracle of revival that followed this deep rejection in Seymour's life. Seymour found another location to meet and the Azusa St. Revival began.

The **SETTING** of the dream-
- A murky pool
- A church

The **CHARACTERS** in the dream-
- Myself
- Lots of people
- Zoe
- William Seymour

The **ACTIVITY** of the dream-
- Talking
- Zoe jumps into the pool
- William Seymour walking to church/ locked out of church

The **FEELINGS** or **EMOTIONS** in the dream-
- Concerned about the dirty water- wanted to see it cleaned
- Afraid for Zoe jumping in
- In awe of the miracle
- Deeply saddened for William
- Recounted the miracle of Azusa after the rejection Seymour experienced and took courage and strength.

Often the interpretation becomes very clear once the dream is broken down in this type fashion. It is best not to get lost in all the details of the dream, but to rather stay with the theme as that is generally where the message is clear. Keeping with the basic facts will help to simplify the interpretation and not allow for becoming bogged down with the interpretation.

What does the dream mean?

- We are on the brink of a spiritual awakening.

Why is Zoe in the dream?

- Zoe means life. God is releasing life into cloudy and mirky waters of our soul.
- Zoe is 8 years old in the dream. The number 8, is a sign to me of new beginnings.
- Zoe is a child and I believe The Lord will stir in the hearts of children to dive in deeper with Him. There are children who will be known as "mystics" in this Awakening.

Why is William Seymour in the dream?

- I love reading about the Azusa St. Revival. William overcame deep betrayal and discouragement.

I already knew who William Seymour was and I also knew about the children who were greatly used in the revival (heightened spiritual awakening, awareness and response among God's people) he was a part of. God was speaking to me through the life experiences of others in my dream.[4]

What is the wisdom of the dream?

Keep walking (William continued walking) - and rehearse what God has done in past days. In the dream I took strength and courage in watching William continuing to walk- and by recounting the miracle of the outpouring of the Azusa St. Revival.

---

[4] http://www.theazusastreetrevival.com/

Timing in a dream.

Sometimes in dreams there is a time given for something to happen. As in prophetic ministry or spiritual readings, we need to understand God's timetable. From a Biblical standpoint, "immediately", "very soon", "this day", or "now is the time" can all translate into the manifestation of the promise being fulfilled days or even years down the road. Be careful of using your own time table.

Basic Rules to Follow in Dream Interpretation-

1- Ask God what He is speaking to you
2- Be accountable with your dreams by writing out the dreams, using a pattern as above, listing the setting, the characters, the activity and the feelings you experienced in the dream.
3- Evaluate emotions you felt in the dream and when you woke up. Ask yourself what emotions you experienced or issues you were facing the day or night before the dream occurred.
4- Search out the meaning of key phrases or symbols in the dream using the Scriptures. A concordance is very helpful in finding names, symbols, etc.
5- Search out the meaning from the natural in understanding what it means to you. Does the dream represent the past, present or future? Some dreams from past events can be a catalyst for healing.
6- Is the dream literal or symbolic? Learn basic symbols to guide and help you in the interpreting of dreams.

7- Is the dream intended for you or someone else? If you are only observing and not active in the dream, it may be for the other person.
8- Keep to the main facts of the dream. Reduce it to the simplest form and then build on it from there.
9- Look for the aha! In the dream. The dreamer will know when the dream makes sense and the interpretation is complete.

CHAPTER IV
WHAT DOES IT MEAN WHEN I DREAM...

Sometimes you will dream with various cities or states or places in your dream. One possibility in helping to find the interpretation is in the definition of that location or in knowing what the city or state is known for. Below are just a few examples-

- Atlanta= secure, immovable
- Canandaigua= chosen place
- Chicago= the windy city, gang activity
- Kentucky= bluegrass state, horse country
- Las Vegas= gambling, sin city
- Los Angeles= city of the angels
- Newburgh= George Washington's headquarters
- New York= a place where dreams are made of (song)
- New York City= the city that never sleeps, mecca of fashion
- Rochester= stone camp or fortress
- Washington DC= politics, history, beautiful buildings, monuments

What if you dream you die suddenly?

Most times, death in dreams represents life and not death. When we die to self, we find freedom. It also suggests that a life changing situation is coming suddenly. It could be that you are dying to something holding you back.

What does it mean to have a dream within a dream?

This type of dream is typically very important. It is the same as when Jesus said, Verily, verily or truly, truly I say unto you. It may deal with a "life call" or message that God does not want you to miss.

What does it mean if I dream of someone?

First ask yourself, what is the basic immediate impression of that person that comes to mind and then ask yourself, what are they doing in the dream that I am doing in real life.

Remember, if the dream is especially centered around that person doing something wrong or needing adjustment, I think it best to apply it to myself.

If the immediate impression of that person is a stubbornness, you will want to see where you are being stubborn.

Why do I dream that I am falling and then wake up?

It could be that your nerves are unwinding. This can be more of a physical condition. It could also mean you feel you have lost control in an area of your life. Most people can remember having this dream at some point in their life. Try to recall as much of the dream as possible to discover clues for the interpretation.

What if I dream that I discover I am naked in public?

This probably means that you are in a vulnerable place. The way you feel in the dream is the key. If you feel embarrassed in the dream then you are probably feeling uncomfortable with something in life. Sometimes you may dream that you are naked but in the dream it seems normal. This occurs as you are at peace with a situation you are facing but still in a place of vulnerability or being seen by others.

What if I dream that a person changes from one person to another?

They (or you) may be in an unstable time in their life or there may be character traits (negative or positive) that you need to assimilate or eliminate.

What if I dream that I am personally hurting or killing someone?

This type dream may alert you to a spirit of jealousy or hatred in your life. It may also speak to the need to deal with a situation. Meditate on the situation in the dream to see if there is a connection to a specific set of circumstances in your life God may be speaking to.

What if two or more people have similar dreams while sleeping under the same roof?

God is clearly speaking to pay attention to the message in the dream.

-God desires to speak to us to give us wisdom. Dreams offer wisdom in a way we may not have been able to hear during our waking hours.

-When something is repeated in Scripture as in Pharaoh's dream (Genesis 41), it is a message you need to give your attention to.

Why do I dream about old boyfriends or girlfriends?

-could be connected to someone currently in your life that is bringing out similar feelings to the ones you felt in the relationship with your former boyfriend/girlfriend and also a possible warning not to make similar mistakes in this relationship

-could be connected to what is being watched on television/movies

-could be connected to what is being meditated on or entertained in thoughts

Dreaming about "old or ex-boyfriends" can represent our relationship with the Lord but these type of dreams can also occur when we entertain thoughts about someone from the past who at one point was a significant part of our life.

The person you dreamt about may not be a part of your life at all in the present. Sometimes we can watch a movie that triggers "feelings" for someone from our past. We must be careful to understand where these dreams come from. The Bible tells us to bring every thought captive. That means if while watching a movie a thought or feeling is triggered in me from a past relationship or feeling I may have had, I need to cast that thought down or it will take root and be destructive in the end. The enemy of your soul would love nothing better than to see you dwelling on past relationships or feelings we may have felt for someone because he knows that if you give attention to those feelings or thoughts you will eventually give yourself to making those thoughts or feelings a reality.

What if I dream about a giraffe?

Sometimes I dream about a certain animal and go online to learn about the characteristics of that animal to help bring the understanding. It is so interesting to learn different facts about animals. Discovering the meaning of a dream can be full of fun and adventure. For example, giraffes sleep less than two hours a day and no more than 5-10 minutes at a time. That speaks to me of watchmen or intercessors who are on alert. Giraffes are exalted in height and see further out. This tells me that God is exalting or raising up the intercessors to see further out. Dreams will overemphasize like a caricature to make a point or give a message.

What if I have a dream that repeats itself?

Usually this will happen if you are missing a message in the dream or it will serve as a reminder of something. The Lord will cause a dream to repeat if we are not catching the message of the dream. This really is to get our attention. Sometimes we will have a dream when we are a child and then have the same dream as an adult. I will give an example-

When my son Josiah was thirteen years of age he had a dream where he was at a playground and a big huge bug was on his arm. The bug had the appearance of a large lobster and the claws were digging into his arm. He screamed for his dad to pull the bug off his arm and his dad came and pulled the bug off.

The interpretation was that something was "bugging" Josiah and all he needed to do was to call on the Father for help.

Twelve years later, Josiah tells me that he has this recurring dream of a bug on his arm and it gets big and multiplies. I told him that he had that dream years ago. The Lord is reminding him to call on Him for help when things bug him.

What if I dream that The Lord tells me who I am going to marry?

Most of the time this kind of dream is revealing your own desires and may not be revealing the desire of the Lord. You should never tell the individual you dreamt about marrying that you had such a dream. When training people in the prophetic ministry I tell them not to prophesy dates or mates and I apply the same principle to dreams. If someone tells you they have a word from The Lord that you are to be their mate, do not give heed as they have something to gain. Our own heart can deceive us. Unfortunately, I have seen others try to use a dream like this as a manipulative tool to gain their own heart's desire and not the Lord's.

Within every dream there is wisdom to glean.

Dreams are like watching a movie while you sleep. Did you know that when you dream, your eyes move rapidly under your eyelids because the dreamer is literally watching a picture? This is called REM sleep.

Sleep is prompted by natural cycles of activity in the brain and consists of two basic states: rapid eye movement (REM) sleep and non-rapid eye movement (NREM) sleep...

During sleep, the body cycles between non-REM and REM sleep. Typically, people begin the sleep cycle with a period of non-REM sleep followed by a very short period of REM sleep. Dreams generally occur in the REM stage of sleep.[5]

Movies bring a message or have a story to tell. Dreams also bring a message. The Lord gives dreams as a means of communicating with us.

---

[5] http://www.webmd.com/sleep-disorders/excessive-sleepiness-10/sleep-101

CHAPTER V
BASIC SYMBOLS

In the process of interpreting dreams, much of what occurs in a dream will be symbolism. A good rule of thumb in discovering what the symbolism might mean is to reduce the activity or object to the simplest form by keeping it simple and personal. Daniel gave the main facts of his dream. I have found this to be helpful in not getting bogged down in thinking there has to be more to the dream. Keep it simple and have fun.

In this section, I will give some basic symbols that I have built in my own understanding of dreams. Many of them can be found in the Scriptures although I will not give references here. I will only list them and you can build from there.

COLORS-

Red: forgiveness, cleansing, justification, redemption, sacrifice, love
    Flip side- Someone red in the face can speak of anger

Green: life, vigor, prosperity, mercy, healing, freshness
    Flip side- Someone green would speak of inexperience/ Green with envy

Blue: revelation, grace, heaven, Holy Spirit, males
    Flip side- Someone feeling blue means they are sad/ Singing the blues

Purple: royalty, kingship, power, majesty, wealth, kingdom

Flip side- Someone turns purple means they are cold or lack oxygen

Yellow: light, joy, celebration, glory, spring

Flip side- Yellow is associated with cowards/ timidity

Silver: redemption, righteousness, wisdom, faith

Flip side- Silver can be an inferior metal

White: purity, surrender, righteousness, peace, glory, without mixture, spotless

Flip side- a little white lie

Black: darkness, mysteries, elegant, classy, lovely

Flip side- evil, the Black Plague

Orange: passion, power, fire, harvest season, fruitfulness, joy

Flip side- brings warning or danger

NUMBERS-

1- beginning, harmony, in a state of agreement, singleness of purpose

2- divide, in the mouth of two witnesses, two are better than one, multiplication

3- strength, fruitfulness, Deity, unity

4- four directions, four seasons, unlimited opportunity, four corners of the earth

5- serve, equipping, start school at age 5

6- man, image, six cities of refuge

7- rest, completion, wisdom

8- new beginnings, covenant

9- 9 Fruits of the Holy Spirit-fruit is grown, 9 Gifts of the Holy Spirit-gifts are given

10- 10 Commandments, judgement, tested, inspection

11- exchange, authority

12- disciples, government

13- time of entering the teen-age years

14- could speak of delay and work

15- Hezekiah had 15 years added to his life- you will be added to
16- sweet 16- innocence
18- time of graduation
21- age of becoming "legal"
30- launching
50- Year of Jubilee
100- hundredfold blessing

Buildings and Places-

Airport= waiting

Attic= past memories, things once used (and may be usable again)

Bank= secure (you can bank on it)

Cafeteria= serving, ministry of helps, teaching

City= busy, highly populated

Country= isolated, quiet, peaceful

Desert= dry, barren, beautiful

Elevator= moving up or down at a fast pace and with little or no effort

Escalator= moving up or down at a slower pace with little or no effort

Front porch= open for everyone to see and open to everyone

High-rise= status, level of calling (where you are at or where you are going)

Hotel= public place of rest or business, temporary dwelling, passing through

House= above the surface- what people see, can be your life, family

Jail= bondage, consequence of sin

Kitchen= place of preparation (training for ministry), pressure (if you can't take the heat, stay out of the kitchen)

Library= knowledge, quiet, please
Mountain= sphere of influence, obstacle
Office building= place where work gets done
Park= rest, leisure, peace, activity, gatherings
Stairways= transition, takes work
Trees= your life
Zoo= confusion (this is like a zoo in here), entertaining children

Transportation-

Bicycles= working at progressing, can speak of the prophetic gift (getting into places that others cannot)
Boats= recreation, spare time, fun

> There are different types of boats and each can have its own meaning and significance. For instance, there are battleships which can speak of a time of war or battle with others. Rowboats can speak of working out, working hard, or spiritual labor.

Bus- takes you from one place to another, it is public transportation meaning shared space and seen by others

Jet- fast method of progress, can be soaring on the wings of the Spirit

Limousine= luxury, fun with people, carries important people

Motorcycle= individualized progress and confidence

Tractor= slow but powerful work

Tractor trailer= people who carry a lot of responsibility

Train= runs on tracks= you are on track

Body-
Arm= strength
Back= backbone, courage
Feet= peace, direction headed
Hand= direction, fellowship
Knees= submission
Legs= strength, support
Neck= the will
Nose= discernment / sticking your nose into other people's business / brown noser
Shoulders= reveal confidence or lack thereof
Teeth= ability to think and digest information. Most of the time when people give me a dream related to teeth, I ask them if they have a difficult relational situation they are facing or a fear of losing a relationship. In almost every case the answer is yes.

The key to understanding symbolism is in thinking about the object in the dream. For instance, oceans are very deep and touch nations. What could it mean if your dream occurred at the ocean? One thought is that God is going very deep in you and touching you with a love for nations. The interpretation obviously depends on the activity in the dream so I am only giving a thought of what it might mean.

Objects-
Back door= the past
Bald tires= inability to gain traction or momentum or inability to grasp or understand
Barbershop= place of removal
Blanket= warmth
Broom= sweeping away the past / witchcraft
Choking= something hindering
Coat= protection, covering of favor

Crops= harvest, deal with time (in due season)
Darts= attack
Dust= neglect
Earthquakes= upheaval
Fence= protection, barrier
Gun= power
Horn= strength
Iron= healing of relationship (ironing out the differences)
Jewelry= treasures
Leaves= temporary covering, nations
Lemon= bad deal
Microscope= close inspection or examination
Mirror= a reflection of what is going on
Mushroom= quick sudden growth, can be poisonous
Nuts and bolts= the essentials
Postage stamp= authority
River= boundary, movement
Road signs- give direction
Rooms= issues of your life
Rug= covering and character
Ruts= habits or addictions, stuck
Sand= improper foundation
Skateboard= balance
Suitcase= temporary and personal
Swimming pool= refreshing
Telephone= communication
Thorns= persecution / protection (hedge of thorns)
Tunnel= passage, way of escape
Volcano= sudden violent reaction to pressure
Weeds= neglect, worry

Creatures- I only list a few as the *"Think Tank"* will get you thinking
Ants= irritation, unwanted guests

Doves= peace
Hamsters= running in circles getting nowhere, caged in
Lady bugs= eat parasites
Leopards= unchanging
Parrots= mimic, copy, mock
Storks= expectancy
Termites= hidden destruction, secret sin

Think Tank
Put your mind to work and fill in the blanks. Have fun.

Bears _____

Beavers _____

Birds _____

Bulls _____

Camels _____

Cats _____

Cattle _____

Chipmunks _____ _____

Deer _____

Dogs _____

Eagles _____

Elephants _____

Fleas _____

Flies _____

Flamingos _____

Foxes _____

Giraffes _____

Goats _____

Hogs _____

Hornets _____

Horses _____

Kangaroos _____

Lambs _____

Mice _____

Moles _____

Monkeys _____

Moths _____

Mules _____

Oxen _____

Peacocks _____

Rabbits _____

Rats _____

Roaches _____

Scorpions _____

Sharks _____

Skunks _____

Snails _____

Swans _____

Tigers _____

Turkeys _____

Turtles _____

Vipers _____

Whales _____

Wolves _____

CHAPTER VI
~Charity's Corner~

Charity is my daughter. Some time ago she had a dream that did prove to be a literal dream about someone else. I asked her to share her dream as an example of how dreams that tend to be literal will bring help to people. I gave her this corner of the book to write. Enjoy!

Dreams. That word alone provokes many thoughts that are based in our own experience. When I look at the impact of dreams in my own life I am thankful. There are times I don't understand my dreams but if I take the time to write them out they usually make sense at some point. Some dreams prepare me for the future, while other dreams help me process emotions and still, others help to bring closure.

I once had a dream about a man who owned a business. In the dream his business was in a house and while he was working, an employee was sneaking into the basement and stealing items from him. I realized I was seeing them but they couldn't see me. I also was aware that the owner had no idea what was taking place.

When I awoke I knew it was for this business owner. God was bringing a warning. I knew that I was going to see this owner that week for an appointment. Because this was only my second time seeing him I didn't know how he might respond to the dream. When I told him the dream he mentioned he had a great staff and didn't really relate to the dream but he did have some things stored in the basement (like in my dream) and hadn't looked down there in a long time. He said no one really knew it was down there so he never worried about checking on it.

About two months later I had another appointment with the owner. He proceeded to thank me for telling him the dream. After our conversation last time he went to the basement to discover some valuable things were stolen and that it was in fact one of his employees in whom he never would have suspected. He was thankful to have caught it when he did because he said it could have been worse.

In this case,, it was only over time that revealed to me that this was in fact a "God dream" and this dream saved this businesses owner from more heartache. Although this individual was not a believer he was willing to hear the dream and in the end, God helped him.

I am a firm believer in dreams for many reasons, including the scriptures that talk about it. But even beyond that I can tell you that dreams have warned me of situations ahead of time related to work, family and relationships. As a result, I have received direction and instruction. I love dreams and looking at them. Dreams take time to process and understand. I wanted to share one of my experiences with a dream and the impact that one dream had on a business owner and eventually on me. Absolutely amazing.

Appendix A
References to Dreams in Scripture

Here are just a few of the references to dreams in the Scriptures.

Genesis 20:3
3 But God came to Abimelech in a dream by night, and said to him, "Indeed you are a dead man because of the woman whom you have taken, for she is a man's wife." NKJV

Genesis 20:6
6 And God said to him in a dream, "Yes, I know that you did this in the integrity of your heart. For I also withheld you from sinning against Me; therefore I did not let you touch her. NKJV

Genesis 31:10
10 And it happened, at the time when the flocks conceived, that I lifted my eyes and saw in a dream, and behold, the rams which leaped upon the flocks were streaked, speckled, and gray-spotted. NKJV

Genesis 31:11
11 Then the Angel of God spoke to me in a dream, saying, 'Jacob.' And I said, 'Here I am.' NKJV

Genesis 31:24
24 But God had come to Laban the Syrian in a dream by night, and said to him, "Be careful that you speak to Jacob neither good nor bad." NKJV

Genesis 37:5
5 Now Joseph had a dream, and he told it to his brothers; and they hated him even more. NKJV

Genesis 37:6
6 So he said to them, "Please hear this dream which I have dreamed: NKJV

Genesis 37:9
9 Then he dreamed still another dream and told it to his brothers, and said, "Look, I have dreamed another dream. And this time, the sun, the moon, and the eleven stars bowed down to me." NKJV

Genesis 37:10
10 So he told it to his father and his brothers; and his father rebuked him and said to him, "What is this dream that you have dreamed? Shall your mother and I and your brothers indeed come to bow down to the earth before you?" NKJV

Genesis 40:5
5 Then the butler and the baker of the king of Egypt, who were confined in the prison, had a dream, both of them, each man's dream in one night and each man's dream with its own interpretation. NKJV

Genesis 40:8
8 And they said to him, "We each have had a dream, and there is no interpreter of it." And Joseph said to them, "Do not interpretations belong to God? Tell them to me, please." NKJV

Genesis 40:9
9 Then the chief butler told his dream to Joseph, and said to him, "Behold, in my dream a vine was before me, NKJV

Genesis 40:16
16 When the chief baker saw that the interpretation was good, he said to Joseph, "I also was in my dream, and there were three white baskets on my head. NKJV

Genesis 41:1
1 Then it came to pass, at the end of two full years, that Pharaoh had a dream; and behold, he stood by the river. NKJV

Genesis 41:7
7 And the seven thin heads devoured the seven plump and full heads. So Pharaoh awoke, and indeed, it was a dream. NKJV

Genesis 41:11
11 we each dreamed a dream in one night, he and I. Each of us dreamed according to the interpretation of his own dream. NKJV

Genesis 41:12
12 Now there was a young Hebrew man with us there, a servant of the captain of the guard. And we told him, and he interpreted our dreams for us; to each man he interpreted according to his own dream. NKJV

Genesis 41:15
15 And Pharaoh said to Joseph, "I have dreamed a dream, and there is no one who can interpret it. But I have heard it said of you that you can understand a dream, to interpret it." NKJV

Genesis 41:17
17 Then Pharaoh said to Joseph: "Behold, in my dream I stood on the bank of the river. NKJV

Genesis 41:22
22 Also I saw in my dream, and suddenly seven heads came up on one stalk, full and good. NKJV

Genesis 41:32
32 And the dream was repeated to Pharaoh twice because the thing is established by God, and God will shortly bring it to pass. NKJV

Numbers 12:6
6 Then He said, "Hear now My words:
If there is a prophet among you,
I, the LORD, make Myself known to him in a vision;
I speak to him in a dream. NKJV

Judges 7:13
13 And when Gideon had come, there was a man telling a dream to his companion. He said, "I have had a dream: To my surprise, a loaf of barley bread tumbled into the camp of Midian; it came to a tent and struck it so that it fell and overturned, and the tent collapsed." NKJV

Judges 7:15
15 And so it was, when Gideon heard the telling of the dream and its interpretation, that he worshiped. He returned to the camp of Israel, and said, "Arise, for the LORD has delivered the camp of Midian into your hand." NKJV

1 Kings 3:5
5 At Gibeon the LORD appeared to Solomon in a dream by night; and God said, "Ask! What shall I give you?" NKJV

1 Kings 3:15
15 Then Solomon awoke; and indeed it had been a dream. And he came to Jerusalem and stood before the ark of the covenant of the LORD, offered up burnt offerings, offered peace offerings, and made a feast for all his servants. NKJV

Job 20:8
8 He will fly away like a dream, and not be found; Yes, he will be chased away like a vision of the night. NKJV

Job 33:14-15
4 For God may speak in one way, or in another, Yet man does not perceive it. 15
15 In a dream, in a vision of the night, When deep sleep falls upon men, While slumbering on their beds, NKJV

Psalm 16:7
7 I will bless the Lord who has given me counsel; My heart also instructs me in the night seasons.

NKJV

Psalms 73:20
20 As a dream when one awakes,
So, Lord, when You awake,
You shall despise their image. NKJV

Psalms 126:1
1 When the LORD brought back the captivity of Zion,
We were like those who dream. NKJV

Ecclesiastes 5:3
3 For a dream comes through much activity,
And a fool's voice is known by his many words. NKJV

Isaiah 29:7
7 The multitude of all the nations who fight against
Ariel, Even all who fight against her and her fortress,
And distress her, Shall be as a dream of a night
vision. NKJV

Jeremiah 23:28
28 "The prophet who has a dream, let him tell a
dream; And he who has My word, let him speak My
word faithfully. What is the chaff to the wheat?" says
the LORD. NKJV

Daniel 2:3
3 And the king said to them, "I have had a dream,
and my spirit is anxious to know the dream." NKJV

Daniel 2:4
4 Then the Chaldeans spoke to the king in Aramaic,
"O king, live forever! Tell your servants the dream,
and we will give the interpretation." NKJV

Daniel 2:5
5 The king answered and said to the Chaldeans, "My decision is firm: if you do not make known the dream to me, and its interpretation, you shall be cut in pieces, and your houses shall be made an ash heap. NKJV

Daniel 2:6
6 However, if you tell the dream and its interpretation, you shall receive from me gifts, rewards, and great honor. Therefore tell me the dream and its interpretation." NKJV

Daniel 2:7
7 They answered again and said, "Let the king tell his servants the dream, and we will give its interpretation." NKJV

Daniel 2:9
9 if you do not make known the dream to me, there is only one decree for you! For you have agreed to speak lying and corrupt words before me till the time has changed. Therefore tell me the dream, and I shall know that you can give me its interpretation." NKJV

Daniel 2:26
26 The king answered and said to Daniel, whose name was Belteshazzar, "Are you able to make known to me the dream which I have seen, and its interpretation?" NKJV

Daniel 2:28
28 But there is a God in heaven who reveals secrets, and He has made known to King Nebuchadnezzar what will be in the latter days. Your dream, and the visions of your head upon your bed, were these: NKJV

Daniel 2:36
36 "This is the dream. Now we will tell the interpretation of it before the king. NKJV

Daniel 2:45
45 Inasmuch as you saw that the stone was cut out of the mountain without hands, and that it broke in pieces the iron, the bronze, the clay, the silver, and the gold--the great God has made known to the king what will come to pass after this. The dream is certain, and its interpretation is sure." NKJV

Daniel 4:5
5 I saw a dream which made me afraid, and the thoughts on my bed and the visions of my head troubled me. NKJV

Daniel 4:6
6 Therefore I issued a decree to bring in all the wise men of Babylon before me, that they might make known to me the interpretation of the dream. NKJV

Daniel 4:7
7 Then the magicians, the astrologers, the Chaldeans, and the soothsayers came in, and I told them the dream; but they did not make known to me its interpretation. NKJV

Daniel 4:8
8 But at last Daniel came before me (his name is
Belteshazzar, according to the name of my god; in
him is the Spirit of the Holy God), and I told the
dream before him, saying: NKJV

Daniel 4:9
9 "Belteshazzar, chief of the magicians, because I
know that the Spirit of the Holy God is in you, and no
secret troubles you, explain to me the visions of my
dream that I have seen, and its interpretation. NKJV

Daniel 4:18
18 "This dream I, King Nebuchadnezzar, have seen.
Now you, Belteshazzar, declare its interpretation,
since all the wise men of my kingdom are not able to
make known to me the interpretation; but you are
able, for the Spirit of the Holy God is in you." NKJV

Daniel 4:19
19 Then Daniel, whose name was Belteshazzar, was
astonished for a time, and his thoughts troubled him.
So the king spoke, and said, "Belteshazzar, do not let
the dream or its interpretation trouble you."
Belteshazzar answered and said, "My lord, may the
dream concern those who hate you, and its
interpretation concern your enemies! NKJV

Daniel 7:1
1 In the first year of Belshazzar king of Babylon,
Daniel had a dream and visions of his head while on
his bed. Then he wrote down the dream, telling the
main facts. NKJV

Joel 2:28

28 "And it shall come to pass afterward
That I will pour out My Spirit on all flesh;
Your sons and your daughters shall prophesy,
Your old men shall dream dreams,
Your young men shall see visions. NKJV

Matthew 1:20
20 But while he thought about these things, behold,
an angel of the Lord appeared to him in a dream,
saying, "Joseph, son of David, do not be afraid to
take to you Mary your wife, for that which is
conceived in her is of the Holy Spirit. NKJV

Matthew 2:12
12 Then, being divinely warned in a dream that they
should not return to Herod, they departed for their
own country another way. NKJV

Matthew 2:13
13 Now when they had departed, behold, an angel of
the Lord appeared to Joseph in a dream, saying,
"Arise, take the young Child and His mother, flee to
Egypt, and stay there until I bring you word; for
Herod will seek the young Child to destroy Him."
NKJV

Matthew 2:19
19 But when Herod was dead, behold, an angel of the
Lord appeared in a dream to Joseph in Egypt, NKJV

Matthew 2:22
22 But when he heard that Archelaus was reigning
over Judea instead of his father Herod, he was afraid
to go there. And being warned by God in a dream, he
turned aside into the region of Galilee. NKJV

Matthew 27:19
19 While he was sitting on the judgment seat, his wife
sent to him, saying, "Have nothing to do with that
just Man, for I have suffered many things today in a
dream because of Him." NKJV

Acts 2:17
17 'And it shall come to pass in the last days, says
God, That I will pour out of My Spirit on all flesh;
Your sons and your daughters shall prophesy,
Your young men shall see visions, Your old men shall
dream dreams. NKJV

JOURNAL YOUR DREAM

DREAM

_____

_____

_____

_____

_____

_____

_____

_____

_____

_____

_____

_____

_____

_____

_____

_____

_____

_____

_____

JOURNAL YOUR DREAM

1- The Setting

_____

_____

_____

2- The Characters

_____

_____

_____

3- The Plot or Activity

_____

_____

_____

4- The Feelings or Emotions in the dream

_____

_____

_____

5- What is the wisdom in the dream

_____

_____

_____

JOURNAL YOUR DREAM

DREAM

_____

_____

_____

_____

_____

_____

_____

_____

_____

_____

_____

_____

_____

_____

_____

_____

_____

_____

_____

_____

_____

_____

JOURNAL YOUR DREAM

1- The Setting

_____

_____

_____

2- The Characters

_____

_____

_____

3- The Plot or Activity

_____

_____

_____

4- The Feelings or Emotions in the dream

_____

_____

_____

5- What is the wisdom in the dream

_____

_____

_____

JOURNAL YOUR DREAM

DREAM

_____

_____

_____

_____

_____

_____

_____

_____

_____

_____

_____

_____

_____

_____

_____

_____

_____

_____

_____

JOURNAL YOUR DREAM

1- The Setting

_____

_____

_____

2- The Characters

_____

_____

_____

3- The Plot or Activity

_____

_____

_____

4- The Feelings or Emotions in the dream

_____

_____

_____

5- What is the wisdom in the dream

_____

_____

_____

JOURNAL YOUR DREAM

DREAM

_____

_____

_____

_____

_____

_____

_____

_____

_____

_____

_____

_____

_____

_____

_____

_____

_____

_____

JOURNAL YOUR DREAM

1- The Setting

_____

_____

_____

2- The Characters

_____

_____

_____

3- The Plot or Activity

_____

_____

_____

4- The Feelings or Emotions in the dream

_____

_____

_____

5- What is the wisdom in the dream

_____

_____

_____

JOURNAL YOUR DREAM

DREAM

_____

_____

_____

_____

_____

_____

_____

_____

_____

_____

_____

_____

_____

_____

_____

_____

_____

_____

_____

_____

JOURNAL YOUR DREAM

1- The Setting

_____

_____

_____

2- The Characters

_____

_____

_____

3- The Plot or Activity

_____

_____

_____

4- The Feelings or Emotions in the dream

_____

_____

_____

5- What is the wisdom in the dream

_____

_____

_____

JOURNAL YOUR DREAM

DREAM

_____

_____

_____

_____

_____

_____

_____

_____

_____

_____

_____

_____

_____

_____

_____

_____

_____

_____

_____

JOURNAL YOUR DREAM

1- The Setting

_____

_____

_____

2- The Characters

_____

_____

_____

3- The Plot or Activity

_____

_____

_____

4- The Feelings or Emotions in the dream

_____

_____

_____

5- What is the wisdom in the dream

_____

_____

_____

JOURNAL YOUR DREAM

DREAM

_____

_____

_____

_____

_____

_____

_____

_____

_____

_____

_____

_____

_____

_____

_____

_____

_____

_____

_____

JOURNAL YOUR DREAM

1- The Setting

_____

_____

_____

2- The Characters

_____

_____

_____

3- The Plot or Activity

_____

_____

_____

4- The Feelings or Emotions in the dream

_____

_____

_____

5- What is the wisdom in the dream

_____

_____

_____

JOURNAL YOUR DREAM

DREAM

_____

_____

_____

_____

_____

_____

_____

_____

_____

_____

_____

_____

_____

_____

_____

_____

_____

_____

_____

JOURNAL YOUR DREAM

1- The Setting

_____

_____

_____

2- The Characters

_____

_____

_____

3- The Plot or Activity

_____

_____

_____

4- The Feelings or Emotions in the dream

_____

_____

_____

5- What is the wisdom in the dream

_____

_____

_____

JOURNAL YOUR DREAM

DREAM

_____

_____

_____

_____

_____

_____

_____

_____

_____

_____

_____

_____

_____

_____

_____

_____

_____

_____

JOURNAL YOUR DREAM

1- The Setting

_____

_____

_____

2- The Characters

_____

_____

_____

3- The Plot or Activity

_____

_____

_____

4- The Feelings or Emotions in the dream

_____

_____

_____

5- What is the wisdom in the dream

_____

_____

_____

JOURNAL YOUR DREAM

DREAM

_____

_____

_____

_____

_____

_____

_____

_____

_____

_____

_____

_____

_____

_____

_____

_____

_____

_____

JOURNAL YOUR DREAM

1- The Setting

_____

_____

_____

2- The Characters

_____

_____

_____

3- The Plot or Activity

_____

_____

_____

4- The Feelings or Emotions in the dream

_____

_____

_____

5- What is the wisdom in the dream

_____

_____

_____

Made in the USA
Charleston, SC
18 May 2014